Bursts of Emotions

By Deborah Jefferson

DEDICATION

This book isn't dedicated to anyone specifically, but to each one of you who may have trouble expressing their emotions. This is a collection of thoughts about life. On this journey of self-discovery, I have encountered many individuals. There are poems about life, love, and loss. As you read through the pages feel the bursts of emotions just as I did. As you go through life ignite an explosion and set off a burst of emotions.

CONTENTS

Amazing Hue

How can you miss something
That you never really had
You thought you had it
Which is sad

Now you're longing for this
Have you ever had anyone
To dream of your kiss
And desire your touch

Will you find someone to love you
Unconditionally and completely
Will they like you when you're
Not feeling yourself or pretty

Someone to hold you on a bad day
Even when your day was good
He takes your breath away
Passionate in every way he could

One day you will find him
He will be waiting for you
And he will be marked with
The   most   amazing   hue

Preserves

Someone just for me
I don't want to share
He'll spend time with me
Always be there

He'll make me laugh
I'll make him smile
Because the love we have
Is just right

He'll understand my needs
Read my thoughts
Be patient with me
Not tell me what I ought

Someone to love me
To like me when it's hard
Someone to trust me

Someone to listen
And really hear
Someone to pay attention
To my all my fears

I will give him my love
That I know he deserves
But for now, that love

Is   in   a   jar   like   preserves

Time For Self

These four walls
Those two windows
That is all
I can think of

My thoughts
My voice
So distraught
Not by choice

Just me alone
No one else
A reflection
Time   for   self

My Forever Someone

My forever someone
Who will he be
Will he be the one
That I think he will be

How will I know him
When will we meet
Will he appear on a whim
A bed of deceit

My forever someone
Will you wait for me
Our time will come
Once I have healed

I can't wait to meet you
Just wait and see
I'll learn how to love you
And show you how to love me

My forever someone
It'll be just you and me
We'll become as one
And get married

Do you even exist
Will you come and then run
Are you worth the risk

My forever someone

The Right Person

Become the right person
For the right reasons
Learn the right lessons
Going through the seasons

Becoming the right person
To be a better me
An improved version
With all the critiques

Becoming the right person
What does that mean
I was wrong for someone
Or so it seemed

Becoming the right person
Steadily growing
Waiting on the right person
Trusting and knowing

Me And You

Getting to know me
After all these years
Who do I really see
When I look in the mirror

I'm looking closely
Taking a long stare
Trying to focus
On the woman in there

I haven't seen her in awhile
She disappeared one day
I missed her smile
I hope she's back to stay

So she can do everything
That she was meant to do
And be a blessing
To me and you

Be Alright

Rips and pains and tears
They are coming from
Everywhere

They sneak up on me
At any given time
And won't let me be

Feels like I'm fine
Then suddenly
Life drops another dime

Time to adjust
Do what I can do
Trust my gut

That's right
I can do this
It will be alright

Wishes

Have I found you
Did it really happen
I didn't think it would happen this soon
But I'm happy

You make me smile
When I think of you
I miss you when it's been a while
Of hearing from you

You say the right things
At the right times
For the right reasons
Or are they just lines

Did you make up a story
Plan it out from start to finish
Get me not to worry
Then take away all my wishes

Ever So Gently

Going through this life now
Trying to find my way
I am still learning how
To say what I want to say

It is like I am learning about me
Every single day
I look in the mirror to see
And I think, no way

You are doing this sis
With God by your side
Sometimes it is hit or miss
But just stay on the ride

You will find your purpose
Just wait patiently
It will come to the surface
Ever so gently
.

The Open Road

Being alone is harder than I thought
At least that is how it seems
But I do enjoy when I drive off
The open road is all that I see

Driving along the country roads
Barely having time to stop and think
All my troubles just seem to unload
Every single time that I blink

Taking this time to reflect on life
So much has happened
There has been so much strife
And so much sadness

Sometimes I see the Great Divide
When I think of my family
Bur when I take that long drive
The open road is all that I see

Loving Me

Loving me enough to say
I want to but I cannot
While wanting you in such a way
With everything I've got

Loving me enough to be
Open and honest
About how you make me feel
Yet still being modest

Loving me enough to do
What I know is right
Even when I don't want to
I must keep up the fight

Loving me enough to know
That I am worthy of more
Taking things slow
In order to soar

Navigatin

Navigatin through this
Trying to figure out my way sis
Sometimes I get so pissed
At the hit or miss

Tell me what it is
To minimize the ish
Let's get to the business
Check off the to-do list

I'm so tired of life
Why is everything a fight
Can it be just right
For just one night

Can I get one day
Where I can play
Or just lay
And relax all day

THE ONE

How did this happen
Who would've thought
That we would meet up again
Is this what we sought

It's been so long
Since we've seen one another
I hear a sweet song
When I think of us together

Was it fate that came to pass
It must be so
Save the best for last
And go with the flow

Can this be real
I've been waiting on you
Have you been waiting on me
Can this really be true

I'm looking forward to the day
When we can become as one
Are we soulmates
Have I found the one

Let Us Know

The way you make me feel
I can't explain it
Can this be real
Or a coincidence

I'm trying to understand this
Was this in the plans
Like divine bliss
Sent from the heavens

We can be the peace
For each other
As our souls connect
With one another

Pour out our love

Let it overflow
If it was sent from above
Lord, please let us know

A Light To This Candle

Why do I care for you so much

I've never even felt your touch

I've heard your voice

By choice

I want to focus my eyes on you

Get lost in you

When will I see you

During the next full moon

I remember you

I swear I do

But I need a refresher

A jolt of fresh air

A match to light

The fire to ignite

A light to this candle

That only you can handle

Am I still In The Whirlwind

What's going on

Where is life taking me

What is this song

Will this be a memory

Is it going to last long

When will it end

Did I do something wrong

Am I still in the whirlwind

Can it die down to a storm

Or just a light wind

Can we just form

A bond from within

That is so strong

It can handle anything

As Big As The Sea

What is going on
I cannot see
As wide as the ocean
As big as the sea

Falling so deep
I'm drowning
Can't place my feet
No foundation

Where is this place
Ten thousand feet below
Is there enough space
Where can I go

Till the water runs
As far as I can see
As wide as the ocean
As big as the sea

Was It All A dream

Was it all a dream
Or my imagination
A fantasy
Maybe a vacation
All in my mind
How could this be
After all this time
It must be reality
Just like sunshine
And the stars in the sky
Everything aligned
And floating on high
Is how it seems
Did I take a flight
Or was it all a dream

Far Away

So far way
How can this be
Someday you say
You and I can be

Living our dream
Side by side
No longer a fantasy
A whole new life

The girl from the water
The guy from another land
Their hearts growing fonder
Tell me what will happen

A Stand

Why'd you have to do that ish
Played with my emotions
You really messed up a sis
What gave you the notion
That you could try me like this
Had me all in my head
A whole new world
So many things were said
Like I was your girl
And you were my man
You really had me going
I guess you had a plan
Maybe you didn't
But I had to take a stand

Prepare Myself

This is killing me

How could this happen

It's like a part of me

Has been broken

You were ripped away

In the blink of an eye

This was the worst day

Of my entire life

Gone with no regard

No chance to think

This new reality

Is starting to sink

How can I fix it

Lord please help

I just need a minute

To prepare myself

The Way

It's dark in here I can't see

Someone turned off the lights

Or was it an entity

I don't even know what to fight

The room had a plain canvas

Then some lines were added

Threw on a few pastels

And texture and shades

As the painting began to dry

The artistry began to fade

Was it just the light

Or is it just the way

The Cycle

Fluctuating temperatures

Rising and falling

A few degrees here and there

The conditions are not evolving

An electric spark that gave a flicker

But the current seemed strong

Or was it just a freak of nature

All along

It's funny how the weather changes

One day it's scorching hot

The next day its cool and rainy

The cycle just doesn't stop

Estranged

Maybe I've never had this

Or maybe that's not it

But being just your friend

Is not what I wanted

I appreciate the thought

Although sometimes I don't

Those feelings that you fought

My mind still won't

How can we be pals

Like nothing ever happened

This might take a while

Now I must re-examine

I can't be what you want

I don't even know what that is

To be your confidant

Or just one of your peers
page

continued on next

Do you even know what you want

Someone to reach out to

Just so you can be nonchalant

Like you don't even have a clue

Either way I must refocus

Put myself first for a change

Since there can be no us

I'll have to become estranged

YOU

I don't want to be an option

Or just the object of your affection

I want all your attention

Not to mention

The fact that I'll give you my all

Should make you feel as tall

As the highest mountain

As if you are someone

That deserves this kind of love

You must be a cut above

Those other people

   Places and things
That seem to be just right

But only for one night

No thank you

I can have better than you

I am better than you

What makes you

Think so highly of you

Thought Of

It's nice to be thought of'

But what are you thinking

It's nice to be sought out

Even offered a trinket

It's nice to be thought of

To want to spend time together

Wear me like a glove

Keep me warm in this weather

It's nice to be thought of

But to be forgotten

Makes you feel unloved

Or even unwanted

It's nice to be thought of

But for how long

Is this just a part of

Another sad love song

Sent From Above

Why do I still think of you
I feel like such a fool
What did you do
I honestly have no clue
Its just something about you
From the first day I knew
That I was for you
And that you
Were sent to me
Like a dream
That was meant to be
Accept we
Had so many things
We were handling
They were getting
In the way of
True love
That was sent from above

Forever

I can't believe you're gone
Why did this happen
I feel like this is all wrong
I don't understand

My heart is broken
Shattered in pieces
But God has spoken
He had his reasons

The times we shared
Were so very special
Our lives were paired
In a strong connection

I'm grateful for the time
That we had together
I realize you weren't mine
To be with forever

Productive

It's an attraction
Maybe a distraction
Of some sort
But I can't afford
To be focused on you
Maybe in a few
Days or weeks
I think I can see things more clearly
Not grow weary
Of the things that are going on
All around me
What I see is
Disaster, corruption, destruction
All I can do is
Focus on being productive

Where is the fun, joy, and laughter
All I see is disaster
I just want to climb into the clouds
And scream loud
Just let it all out
But that's no way to live
I must
Keep a strong will
Because life is still
Going on
The days just seem so long
Everything is going wrong
But still, I will
Focus on being productive

Awakened

The night your life forever changed
How could you endure so much pain
Why haven't you gone insane
Hiding your tears in the rain

This can not be real
You don't know how to feel
All you know is that it will
Be hard to heal

He was your heart
At least a big part
You knew from the start
That he was a work of art

Someone so special
With so much potential
A life so precious
He left an impression

How could this happen
At that moment
Are you dreaming
When you will be awakened

Make It Through

This is the hardest thing
I've ever had to do
But it can't be as hard
As what you're going through

I feel so selfish
Missing you so much
But it's overwhelming
Not having your touch

Or hearing your voice
I could listen to you all day
It would be an easy choice
Taking in every word you say

My heart is hurting
And I'm sure yours is too
This feeling is unnerving
But I'm trusting we'll make it through

Why

Why'd you have to treat me so well
Why couldn't you be like the rest
Why couldn't you put me through hell
Why'd you have to be the best

Why'd you have to ask for my number
Why'd you have to call me everyday
Why'd you you make me wonder
Why'd you even stay

Why'd this have to happen
Why didn't God stop us
Why'd it have to be the wrong timing
Why'd we have to rush

Why'd he have to go
Why'd you have to be hurt
Why'd it have to be so
Why'd it have to occur

Sunset

Energy
Shared space
What you give me
At the same pace
What you feel
I can feel the same way
It can be a beautiful thing
Like the waves
In the ocean
Or the sunset
At the end
Of a long day
Or an explosion
So big and loud
That surpasses sound
But you can hear it so clearly
That you are fearfully
Wondering what happened
To this beautiful thing
Then you become saddened
And wishing
Hoping and praying
For that
Beautiful
Sunset

Never Knew

It doesn't have to be all or nothing
but it can be something
But what then
Can it be just you and me
let's just see
It doesn't have to be
A bed of roses
all I know is
We can't be divided
or one-sided
Communication is pertinent
Understanding with intent
In order to make it
Through this maze
Without being phased
Some days
Will be filled with joy
Because of all the ways
You make my heart feel
While other days will be
Filled with heat
Then quenched
With such a coolness
You never knew existed

This Road

Focusing on me

Should've been doing this

I see

Should've put more emphasis

On just doing me

What does that mean

Being with you made me happy

So wasn't I focused on me

Happiness is important

But it simply isn't enough

From now on I can't

Focus on that stuff

Gotta start with a plan

From beginning to the end

Can't go down this road again.

That Other Place

Trying not to go back to heartbreak hotel
 Been there a few times
When I tripped and fell
In love or whatever it was
 I don't know what happened
Because you and me
Were supposed to be
Rockin forever but then never
So, I'm like whatever
 I'm not going back to heartbreak hotel
I would rather go straight to hell
So, when I find myself heading in that direction
 I say to myself
 You gotta be your own protection
Remember you're looking for perfection
Everybody's version is different
Every soul has an imprint
Gotta look deeper than what you see
Look for the seed that planted the tree
Maybe then you'll find the key
To that other place
That has your peace

Foundation

I'm not a Gold-digger
I'm a go getter
seeing you on your grind
helps me stay focused on mine
Every now and then I may lose track of time
but you better believe I'm always gonna get mine
You see I can't associate myself with someone who can't
figure   it out
I'm trying to find what this life is all about
Don't have time to sit around waiting to be found
Find me and let me see if you're worth disturbing my peace
Or will you bring calm to this storm and help me form
A foundation so strong
Nothing could go wrong

Spark

I don't know what's up with you
me and you were supposed to be cool
that's how it was supposed to be
But everyone breaks the rules
I'm no fool
I can go to work all day
and then come out and play
whats that you say
Do I have time to spend with you
that may be true
But I can find a million things
To do instead
Chilling is something I know how to do
And relaxing just like you said
This can be done in many ways
Can you feel the heat from the sun rays
Sending you the vibrations
From the temptation
But then you'll get a cool sensation
From my self-expression
Cold as ice with a spark
Of aggression

What We Found

Did our paths change are we no longer going in the same direction

is there a new set of instructions

that don't include affection or communication

Baby show me the way I'll follow your lead

If you don't know what to say Just let your feelings bleed

I can take it I can deal

Let me be your medicine

 and help you heal

I can be your drug of choice every time you hear my voice

Running through your mind As you try to unwind

We just need to find a common ground

and remember what we found

With Me

I want to know your deepest thoughts your fears
 I want to know all about you
even if you shed tears
 I want to feel your mind
I want to know what's inside
Include me into your world
 make me feel like I'm yours
and you are mine

I want to know who you are without me
So that I know who you are when you're with me
I wanna share all my secrets with you
Let you into the deepest parts of my mind my heart and soul

I want to climb to the mountaintop with you
explore the forest with you
go underwater with you
 till were both grasping for air

Is that too much to ask
I think it's only fair
because when I share
the delicate pieces of me
when you allow me to be free
 Then you'll see that you can be
one with me
at peace with me
in harmony with me
fall in love with me

Full Filled

I kept thinking it was just me

Or that God was slowing things down

But God was showing me

What you were really about

Every time I got a sign

I never even saw it

 Seems like I was blind

Or waiting for something big

You stepped up your game

Played your position

Stated you r claim

And began your mission

Whoa

I'm tired of niggas saying they love me

When all they wanna do is just f$%! me

You say you love me, then show me

I'm worth more than diamonds and rubies

Give me all of you and you'll see the true me

Stop playing with my emotions

And keep it real with me

You gonna bring out the other side of me

The one you're not gonna like

Because she's fighting for me

See were one in the same

Trying to stay sane

While you're playing this game

So stop waisting my time

I was doing just fine

And I can do it again

I can be on my own fly solo

I'm not sitting back waiting to see when

But its gonna hit you like whoa

Can't Let Go

Stop stressing

Don't think about nothing

Gotta think about something

Can't forget about living

What are you getting

Out of life

Are you winning

What does that even mean

Are you losing

Sometimes that's how it seems

Make it go away

Asking and praying

Just keep weighing

So heavy on me sometimes

I feel like I can't breathe

I'm deep in the ground a seed

Trying to grow

Continued on next page

But do we ever stop growing and learning

We're not all knowing

Life definitely keeps showing

Know no matter how bad it gets

I can't let go of it

Remember

Let it be what it's going to be

when its going to be what it's meant to be

why you gotta make it into something that you think it's supposed
to be

just enjoy being able to be you

Not focusing on who

You thought you had to be

or this image they had of you

Just enjoy the moment be open

You never know what life is

going to give you at any point in time

Just stay on your grind keep pushing hard and remember what you
started

All In Stride

I guess I feel what my mother feels

I don't know how to take it

Life is really getting real

I guess there's a first for everything

I can honestly say it stings

I knew this day would come eventually

Isn't it a part of life plan

It's great being an empty nester

Till one day you look around

And there's no other sound

Yeah, you enjoy the peace and quiet

But sometimes you miss the riots, the back-and-forth,

Isn't it supposed to be your time now

What are you complaining about

Live it up, enjoy your life

Just take it all in stride

Grenade

Had me swimming in a sea of emotions

I didn't know if I was coming or going

You opened up my mind

And then froze it in time

I want to go on this journey with you

Be the one to make you smile

Let me feed off your energy

For a while

I love your style

Your whole thought process

My mind body and soul

You can possess

Are we still vibrating off the same frequency

Tell me does your soul even remember me

Is this a connection that will never fade

A slow spark waiting to explode like a grenade

Within

This sounds crazy right

Like trying to see with no sight

But everything is not black-and-white you got to look at

The gray areas

Don't just focus on the exterior

Pay attention to the interior view

That's where everything is

The important stuff that really matters

Let's get serious

When I knock on the door

I need you to let me in

Deep within

Your soul that is

And when I'm there

Let down all your inhibitions

Because baby I'm on a mission

To take you higher than you've ever been

Some might even call it a sin

But my light just turned on from within

Tomorrow

Push past the pain

Find your sunshine in the rain

This world has so much to offer

its insane

It's not gonna find you

Like hide and go seek

They say only a few

will reach their peak

I don't believe that

we all can get to where is its at

But everyone's road

Isn't all flat

Got bumps and holes and cracks

Twists and turns

Either way you go is a lesson learned

What you take from the lesson is up to you

Each day is a time to renew

Continued on next page

Wake up to the morning dew

It's time to reflect on what you've been through

But don't wallow in sorrow

Focus on tomorrow

Unexpected Blessing

You came in like a thief in the night saying and doing everything
just right

God was really listening to my prayers

I want to peel back all the layers

get to know the real you

how can you be so in tune

With my mind body and soul

your warmth is bringing me out of the cold

but still giving me chills like I'm in the snow

It's funny how things happen

like an unexpected blessing

Perfectly imperfect

I'm perfect just the way I am

Judge me how you want

But again, this is who I am

Like me or love me or hate me

But don't mistake me

For someone else

I'm going to be who I am till the day I die

Only I have to live with that for myself this is my life

To live we all, have free will

I understand I have no ill intentions towards you

I have nothing but love for you

And I hope you have the same for me

But mutual respect is what we

should have for one another

We gotta stop judging one another

just because we care for each other

Start looking at the whole picture

maybe even take a look in the mirror Continued on next page

and reflect on your life

Dissect your own anatomy

Open up for the world to see

and maybe we can agree

That life is about being free

Perfectly imperfect that's me

Shatter

Let's talk about so-called friends

I remember when

A friend was someone who you could depend

Trust them with your life

Not have to worry about them doing things out of spite

Where are the real friends that only want to see you win

The ones you know love you

Regardless of what you do

Just be careful when choosing your friends, don't let Anyone latch onto you and play for a fool

Show them you have a strong tool That can fight all your Battles

With a Force so strong all the glass will shatter

I am a self-published author. A mother to three amazing adults and a grandmother to two wonderful grandchildren. I love to write and spend time by the water.

Made in United States
Orlando, FL
11 June 2024

47726361R00036